Spaceman Africa the Musical

Spaceman Africa the Musical by Spaceman Africa
Published by Spaceman Africa © All rights reserved
Book artwork by Kieron Pratt and Aliosa Tran Phan

The moral right of the author has been asserted. All rights reserved. Without limiting the rights under copyright restricted above, no part of this publication may be reproduced, stored in or introduced into a retrieval system, or transmitted, in any form or by any means (electronic, mechanical, photocopying, recording or otherwise), without the prior written permission of the copyright owner of this book. The views of the author belong solely to the author and are not necessarily those of the publisher or the publishing service provider.

[1st Edition 2018, paperback.
ISBN: 978-1-925764-23-9
Publishing services by: PublishMyBook.Online

A catalogue record for this book is available from the National Library of Australia.

Spaceman Africa
the
MUSICAL

Spaceman Africa

Contents

Who is Spaceman Africa?....................7
   Song lyrics: Who is Spaceman Africa?....29
Bondage Bob.............................32
   Song lyrics: Bondage Bob................37
The Horny German Truck Driver 39
   Song lyrics: Horny German Truck Driver .45
The Mel & Junior Stand..................47
   Song lyrics: The Mel & Junior Stand 53
Brian Oliver 55
   Song lyrics: Brian Oliver 65
Did you know you only get ten minutes?....67
   Song lyrics: Did you know you only
   get ten minutes?.......................73
It's on FIRE!............................75
   Song lyrics: It's on FIRE! 83

Sweet Derrière 85
  Song lyrics: Sweet Derrière 89
I don't like Cricket........................92
  Song lyrics: I don't like Cricket..........97
The Cat's Mole 99
  Song lyrics: The Cat's Mole 102
Whiteboard Rafting......................104
  Song lyrics: Whiteboard Rafting.........112
New Orleans Merry-go-round 114
  Song lyrics: New Orleans
  Merry-go-round.......................125

Who is Spaceman Africa?

29th August 2002

"Hi, I'm ringing on behalf of Sean Lewis." Jeremy continued, "Yes, well, you know how he travelled to Dublin for the weekend?"

"Yes," replied my employment agency consultant.

"Well, he was involved in a car accident on Sunday and died this morning."

It's not every day you fail to show up for work and one of your mates phones your boss to tell them you're dead. But, that's what happened when I found myself on a bender with some mates in Donegal, Ireland, when, really, I should have been at my warehouse job in London. At the time of the call, I was alive and well enjoying a few beers in a pub with some local women we'd met the night before. I was having too good a time to return to work. It was this bender that was the death, all be it fake, of Sean Lewis and the birth of Spaceman Africa.

Two months earlier, in June of 2002, I had returned to live and work in London after nine months away in Australia and the US. I found a job through an employment agency, working with Harvey Nichols in Greenford. My job was a typical picker/packer position. I picked orders of food and drink products and then packed them in boxes to be transported to stores throughout the country. I enjoyed the job. It was easy; it was a short ride from home; I was becoming good friends with the other workers, and the supervisors had explained their plans to have me moved to an easier position, working in the wine section. After having been there a few weeks, they produced a roster that extended for six months until January 2003. I remember feeling weird having my future mapped out like that. I liked to move from place to place a lot; who were they to say what I'd be doing in six months? I needn't have worried. To this day, they still think I'm dead.

When the changeover of the two rosters occurred, it worked out in my favour, and I ended up with a week off. I had friends from the States coming over to visit Ireland that same week, so I organised to go over and spend the weekend with them in Dublin. My mate, Jeremy Brown (not real name), who was living in Belfast, was also going to join us.

We all met at our hotel in Dublin, and even though some of us were meeting for the first time, we all got on great. My friends and I were big drinkers, so the weekend in Dublin was somewhat of a blur to me, but I do remember some of the absolute craziness we got up to.

Because Jeremy and I had been to Dublin before, we left the others to do their own thing during the day. We'd all meet up again in the afternoon and then go out together at night. One day, when the others were at the Guinness Factory, Jeremy and I were in a pub drinking, as you do, and Jeremy was explaining how it's possible to change your name and obtain a deed poll on the internet. As a laugh, he once bought a deed poll, changing his mate Pete's name to Edgar Stuart without telling him. Can you imagine Pete's surprise when the deed poll arrived in the mail?

So, I said, "If it's that easy, why don't we change our names?"

And so, it was decided; we were going to change our names. But what's the point of going to all that trouble to change your name if you're going to change it to something common, like Paul Smith? So, we decided on unusual names, but nothing sprung to mind. Weeks later, Jeremy came up with the idea I change my name to my bracelet. I had a bracelet from South Africa that in different coloured beads read S. AFRICA. Jeremy suggested I be Stanley or Siegfried Africa. I said, "Fuck that. I'll be Spaceman Africa."

Spaceman was my nickname years earlier when I worked at the Shepherd's Bush Empire in London. And Spaceman starts with 's'. So, on 25th October 2002, I went to the internet café, Revelations, in Shaftsbury Square, Belfast, with a few friends and changed my name on the internet. The deed poll arrived by mail, a few days later. In the meantime, my partner in crime decided to change his name to Crazy Horse Invincible.

So, I e-mailed my friends about my name change.

G'day All,

just a quick message to let you know that this week I changed my name by deed poll to Spaceman Africa, so if you could all refer to me as that from now on, I'd be most grateful. Hope to hear from you all soon,

Laugh Spaceman

Some of their reactions were quite funny. My friend Paddy, from South Africa, asked if I had lost my marbles and suggested now that I was a spaceman, I would have to watch out for Mulder and Scully: X Files Investigators. My buddy, Fosters, who I knew from London, was straight to the point, "What on earth are you on about son?" My friend Tracy, from Canberra, had a similar question, although she used the word hell instead of earth. "Hello, I love you with all my heart, but what the hell are you talking about?" My mate, Graeme, from Washington DC, assumed dementia had set in.

As you may have guessed, my name is Spaceman Africa. I was born in Sydney, Australia, May 1974, and at the age of four was relocated to the Canberra area, Australia's capital city. I grew up there as a wee lad; I went to school there and worked a few jobs after that but nothing serious. I took the weekends seriously though and enjoyed getting on the piss with my friends and experiencing moments of pure hilarity. We used to write an account of our antics on the bottle of Southern Comfort we had devoured that night.

In my late teens and early twenties, music was a big part of my life. I played the guitar and tinkered on the piano a bit, but my favoured instrument was the bass guitar. Originally, I learnt the guitar, but after the scores of gigs I went to once I was over 18, I saw some bass players whose presence on stage was suave and smooth. They played an important role in the rhythm of the band but stood back, out of the spotlight, happy to play the supportive role. The bass player is the introvert and kind of like the guardian of the band, standing back and keeping their cool, whilst the guitarists parade around like chickens with their heads chopped off. This character type suited my personality and so it wasn't long before I gravitated to the bass. Plus, the bass sound is just cool anyway, not to mention a lot of chicks play bass.

I played in a few bands with different friends, and one of the more interesting groups I played in were Insomnia, an all-male, five-piece rock band. Phill on vocals worked for the Government but wasn't allowed to tell us what he did, as it was confidential. Mick, on guitar, sold toilets for a living; Richie, also on guitar, was a Paralympian, and Tom on drums was a dealer. Whenever stuck for conversation with Tom, I just asked when his next court hearing was coming up. Richie often travelled overseas to compete in various power lifting championships and trials. There was talk that Phill and I would join him on a trip to the States in '96, but nothing ever came of it.

That desire to travel stayed with me, however, and, in 1997, at the age of 22, with nothing tying me to Canberra, I decided to travel the world... first stop London.

I went on that trip without any vaccinations and I caught the travel bug, big time. 20 years, six continents and over 40 countries later, I'm now based in Canberra again. Over that time, I met some amazing people, visited some exciting places and experienced many adventures, some of which were amazing, and others somewhat unfortunate that now, with hindsight, I can see are quite comical. The stories in this book feature a few of the memorable anecdotes I've accumulated over the years. The accompanying CD (or digital album) contains songs relating to these stories.

Continuing on the theme of my name change:

Leading up to Christmas of 2004, I was excited about the four weeks' worth of travel I had coming up, including spending some time over the Christmas and New Year period in Eastern Europe. A whole gang of us were going to meet up in Prague for some fun and frivolity, including my mate Crazy Horse. Crazy's attempts to book a flight, however, hit a bit of a snag and, subsequently, Crazy Horse and I made the news worldwide.

Saturday 4th December 2004

Google search: *ABC Crazy Horse Spaceman*

Here you can read one of the many articles

that went viral on the internet. To find other versions, google: *Jeremy turns crazy* and/or *He's plane crazy: Crazy Horse Invincible*

I was checking my email on the morning of the 7th and noticed a message from my mate, Dan, back in Canberra. The subject line read: Crazy Horse is famous. Dan had been made aware of the ABC article and passed it on to me. I was blown away. Picture Michael J. Fox at the beginning of the first *Back to the Future* movie when he strums his electric guitar that's plugged into a super-charged amplifier and he gets thrown back off his feet about ten metres. That's how blown away I was.

I rang Crazy Horse, "Hey mate, are you aware of this?"

He told me, a few weeks earlier, he was at home snoozing after working a nightshift when he received a phone call from a woman regarding a flight he'd booked online with Jet2.com. The woman was with the bookings department and wanted some answers regarding Crazy's name. She was very aggressive and pushy, demanding to know what his real name was. Having been woken up and then being rudely interrogated, Crazy Horse was not in the most magnanimous of moods. He snapped back, declaring that it *is* his real name. The woman became irate and said that if he didn't give his real name the ticket would be cancelled.

Crazy Horse retaliated, "Listen, it is my real name. It's the name on my passport." And with that, he was asked to go to the airport to prove it.

He also received a phone call from a guy called Adrian who was part of Jet2's PR department. He wanted to do a write-up about Crazy Horse and his name, for the in-flight magazine. Crazy Horse told him the story behind the name change and of other benders he and I had been on and Adrian found it all rather amusing. As a result, Adrian offered us both free flights. When Crazy Horse went to the airport to prove his ID, they took photos of him in front of a plane with his passport and toothbrush, for the in-flight magazine. Crazy Horse was hoping that they'd let him on board and give him a free ride somewhere, but no.

It turned out that Adrian was originally from the Middlesbrough area, just like Crazy Horse and that they both supported the Boro football team. That's where the football reference comes from. I was flying to Prague from London with EasyJet and, as the article reports, I had no trouble securing my seat.

The news article went viral. It appeared in newspapers and magazines, and on webpages all around the world. We had friends from all over, telling us in which obscure publication they had seen the article. At the time, if you were to put 'Crazy Horse and Spaceman' into a search engine, hundreds of results would come up of pages and pages of discussion forums with people posting comments about our names and the article. You can still find a few if you google: *FARK Crazy Horse Invincible*

* * *

In January of 2005, I moved back to Australia after living in the UK for nearly three years. When I'd left Australia years earlier, I left with my original birth name. Now, I was returning with a crazy off-the-wall title. In the first few weeks, I caught up with a few friends in the privacy of their homes, but I hadn't been out on the town yet, socialising with strangers, to introduce Canberra to my new name. Canberrans can be quite conservative so I wasn't sure how they'd react to the name Spaceman Africa. I thought they'd probably think I was a weirdo or stupid.

The first dealings I had with the community

were with various government departments to alert them of my name change. The name evoked many different responses, from laughter to disbelief and denial ("I'm not calling you that"), through to total acceptance. Because of the name Africa, when I showed up to appointments, many people were expecting a black man with dreadlocks and were surprised when a shaven-headed, white man showed up.

My name got questioned a lot over the phone. "Africa? As in the country?" If they were polite and friendly, I'd say yes. But if they were being rude and unaccepting of my name, then I'd put them in their place and correct them. "No. Africa as in the continent."

Some people thought it was my name since birth and asked about its origin. I used to answer that it was a Northern Irish name. Others asked, "Your parents must have been hippies when you were born, were they?" I replied, "I don't know; I can't remember. I was quite young when I was born."

Whilst I'd been away, friends of mine had built up the legend of Spaceman Africa and relayed stories to their friends and work colleagues of the numerous adventures I'd experienced. When I met them, many of them expressed their surprise and disappointment to discover that I was a nerd. My attitude was, "Well, fuck you." It put me off meeting friends of friends. If someone said, "My friend wants to meet you. I've told them all about you," I invariably knew I wasn't going to live up to expectations.

Towards the end of 2005, it came to my attention that other people were using my name. Various people were using Spaceman Africa as their username on internet gaming sites and/or profile pages. That didn't bother me so much but there were a few cases of my name being used as a band name—Crazy Horse's too. There were bands called Spaceman Africa in Young, NSW; Weston-Super-Mare, UK; and in Michigan, USA. There was a band called Crazy Horse Invincible in Sydney and, in the States, there was a group combining the two: Spaceman Africa & The Invincibles.

This did piss me off.

I didn't go to all that trouble to come up with an original name just for other people to use it.

I was also worried about what might happen if they were to become successful. People might think I got my name from the band. I paid the mandatory $260 to apply to the Australian Government to register the name as a trademark with the intention of applying internationally after that. The government rejected my application and I lost the $260 in the process. Ah, well. Life happens.

Today, people using my name doesn't bother me so much. Thankfully though, none of those bands achieved any success. My favourite story regarding the use of my name comes from Massachusetts, USA. A woman sent me an email telling me that my name was legend in her office at work. Her work colleague's unborn child was nicknamed Spaceman Africa. They had seen my story in a baby book. When the boy was born, and christened Drew, they still called him by his nickname.

I didn't understand at first what she was referring to when she said 'baby book'. I found out years later that there's a book of 10,000 baby names. As well as lists of suggested names, it has funny and interesting stories in the margins and the story of Crazy Horse and me, taken from the Jet2 article, is one of them.

In March of 2008, I was minding my own business when I received an email from my friend, Miss Kylie J, in Melbourne, telling me she'd just voted for my name on a website called Name of the Year

Voted for my name? What the hell is she on about? Naturally, I clicked on the link and landed on a webpage that was to become my second home for the next four weeks. To my surprise, and amusement, my name was part of a name of the year competition. I discovered that a group of 'great names' aficionados, from an Ivy League University in the States, had been running a name competition each year since 1983, which is still running as of 2017.

The Name of the Year (NOTY) High Committee find the names and nominate them for the NOTY ballot. They discovered my name from the Jet2 article. For some reason, Crazy Horse wasn't nominated.

There are two winners each year. One winner is voted for by the public and the other is voted for by the NOTY High Committee. The ballot starts with 60 names, all of which are real. One name goes up against another and the public vote for their favourite name and the winner is the name with the most votes. That name then goes on to the next round whilst the loser is knocked out of the competition.

When I stumbled upon the competition, my name had already progressed to the third round of voting. But, once I realised what was going on, I asked everyone I knew to get involved and to vote for me. If you go onto the website, www.nameoftheyear.com, and scroll down a bit. On the right-hand side, under 'NOTY Archives', you can still access the 2008 ballot and see some of the names I was up against. Some of my favourites are Thankgod Amaefule, Bridget Midgett, Johnny Moustache, Queen Lovelady and LaWanna Holiday. Interestingly, there was another entrant with the same surname as me—Free-King Africa. And there was also someone called Danger Guerrero. It's a cool name but everyone should know that 'danger' is a middle name, not a first name. J

I had comfortably beaten Da'veed Dildy in the first round and Silky Labie in the second.

By the time I had become aware of the competition, I was on my way to defeating Urban Couch in the third round. Once victory was mine against Urban Couch, I had progressed to the final eight names. I was then up against the top seed in my group; Destiny Frankenstein. This campaign was to become the most epic battle of the whole competition.

From what I remember, each round of voting lasted a couple of days. The rules were only one vote per person per round. Once I'd made my vote (I voted for myself, of course, hahaha), I contacted all my friends and encouraged them to vote for me. It's not easy motivating people to do something, especially more than once. Many of my friends pointed out that they had already voted for me. I thanked them but explained that that was in the last round. A new round had started and I needed their vote again. And bless 'em, my friends, and friends of friends, got behind me and gave me a fighting chance of advancing to the next round.

But Destiny Frankenstein had a lot of support, including from the NOTY High Committee. In their daily blog posts, the committee were advocating Destiny and, halfway through our melee, the High Committee announced that Destiny Frankenstein had won the 2008 NOTY Committee vote. Based on their write-up, Destiny Frankenstein was a 25-year-old woman from Oklahoma, USA, a keen baseball player and had a younger sister named Cherish. The High Committee congratulated me on following through on a drunken vow and changing my name but, because of the unintended absurdity of the name Destiny Frankenstein, she was their favourite and they made no secret about it either.

Hundreds of votes were made. Our match-up generated by far the most votes and was the closest run contest so far of any of the previous rounds. The High Committee had announced a date and time that the voting would close. I don't know about Destiny, but I was hounding all my family and friends to vote, if they hadn't already. It was close. Each of us had over 600 votes. Over the previous few days, we'd swapped back and forth in leading the votes but, when the cutoff time for voting arrived, Destiny had more votes than I did.

But, something weird happened. In the earlier rounds, when the cutoff time had arrived, the competition organisers took down the voting page from the website so that it wasn't possible to vote anymore. In this instance, the voting page stayed up and voting was still 'live'. Voting stayed open for another 40 minutes before the voting page was taken down. And guess what? In those extra minutes, I had snuck in front to win by seven votes.

"WOOHOO! In your FACE, High Committee."

I was pumped. The weight after a tense few days had now been lifted. After such an intense battle, I wanted to go on and win the public vote title. I had now made it to the final four. Too much time and effort had been put into getting this far, to then get knocked out in the finals. Plus, I wanted to win to piss the High Committee off. Celebrations were short lived as the next round of voting got underway a day or two later. My opponent in the next round was Phyllis Mangina; the winner would go on to fight for the title in the final.

After the battle with Destiny Frankenstein, the next round was somewhat of an anti-climax. I don't remember much about it, which tells me it wasn't that memorable. From what I do remember, I won quite comfortably and advanced to the final to compete against… Fonda Dicks.

Fonda Dicks proved to be a tough opponent, as well. According to the NOTY blog, she was a woman born in the 50s in Iowa, USA, and was well-known as a high school girls basketball star. The final attracted a lot of votes too, but it wasn't as close or tense as the battle with Destiny. When it was daytime in Australia and people were sleeping in the States, I tended to gain more votes. Whilst Australia was sleeping, Fonda Dicks always gained more votes. It seemed like the High Committee had lost all interest now that their golden child, Destiny Frankenstein, was out of the competition. There were less blogposts from them commentating on the contest. Once again, it was a bit anti-climactic and my fans voted me the winner by more than 100 votes.

I was now winner of the 2008 Name of the Year People's Division. I was elated and thanked all my friends and family for making the victory possible. I didn't win anything of material value for coming first but I won the honour and bragging rights. Ever since, when my name has come up in conversation, it's been great to tell people that my name was voted 2008 name of the year.

The NOTY High Committee eventually recognised my victory the next day after the polls had closed with an entertaining write-up, including some of the comments written by my supporters. Google: Spaceman Africa is 2008 name of year

The people had spoken, indeed.

Who is Spaceman Africa?

Lyrics:

There once was a man who changed his name
His name went viral and brought acclaim
A deed poll online
And a shift in time
And his life was never the same

There once was a man named Space
His name from birth became erased
He and Crazy Horse
They have no remorse
They're known all over the place

Spaceman Africa
He's a man of a different calibre
Born and raised in Australia
Living the dream in Canberra

Spaceman Africa
He's a charming bachelor
Bought a bracelet in South Africa
And changed his name from Angela
Nah, just kidding. It was Pamela
No, seriously, it was Erica

There once was a name contest
To choose which name was the best
It's a funny anecdote
How Space won the vote
Poor Fonda Dicks was not so blessed

There once was a budget airline
Who questioned if Crazy was genuine
He had to show ID
So they'd leave him be
But Space booked his seat just fine

Spaceman Africa
He plays guitar like an amateur
His guns are spectacular
Said no one ever

Spaceman he's a traveller
But he ain't no drug trafficker
He ain't no troublemaker
And ladies, he's a great lovemaker

Africa? As in the country
Nah mate, what I think it is you meant
Was Africa like the continent.

Spaceman Africa
Snowman Antarctica
Sandman Arabia
Swagman Australia
Superman America
Sheikhman Algeria
Sovietman Armenia

Bondage Bob

Ever been stuck as to what to buy someone for Christmas? For example, what *do* you buy a seven-month-old baby? I guess you could buy something that is helpful to the parents. I'm a childless male; I have no idea what new parents want or need. I do know this though. They don't need an uncle giving their child a sex slavery themed toy.

I had arrived back in my home town of Canberra, in late 2001, after ten months travelling around Europe. I decided I would stay for the summer, which included Christmas. This particular Christmas, my brother, Neville, invited me to have Christmas lunch at his house. Also invited was his wife's family, including her parents, grandparents, her sister and sister's husband.

The in-law's presence indicated that the day was going to be quite a formal affair. The grandparents were going to be old and harmless, but the mother-in-law was the stereotypical mother-in-law and I could only imagine the pain in the butt she was going to be.

My brother had a 7-month-old boy, called John Robert, experiencing his first Christmas and so it was expected that everyone would buy a present for the young man. Now, I like to be a little different to everyone else. I'd spoken to a few people regarding their choice of gift and they had taken the soft option of buying a cuddly toy for JR. Not me, I thought. But the closer the 25th loomed, the more desperate I became and I found myself taking the easy way out and buying the young lad a stuffed bear.

But if I thought Christmas day was going to be boring and uneventful, I changed all that with a gift that was sure to raise a few eyebrows. I bought JR a small teddy bear ... dressed ... in bondage wear. Bondage Bob was his name. He was dressed in leather undies and was tied up with leather straps. He even had a ball gag in his mouth with leather straps around his head.

Before you start thinking I'm a weird, sick puppy, I didn't go out shopping specifically to buy a bondage toy. I stumbled across the bear when browsing through a novelty shop. As soon as I saw it, I burst out laughing. I knew immediately that my present search was over. I couldn't help but laugh thinking about the trouble I was going to cause when the in-laws saw what I was to give their grandson. The bear even came with a tag attached to it containing a poem. You can hear the poem in the bridge of the song. I thought I may never be invited to another one of their Christmas lunches again.

Christmas day arrived and my brother's wife, Belinda, cooked some great food. Belinda had been preparing the meal since lunchtime the day before. For starters, we had prawns and orange duck. For the main meal, we had some lovely turkey with roast potatoes and vegies all covered in gravy—delicious. All nine of us present enjoyed the tasty food and ate far too much.

As for Bondage Bob, well, after John woke from his afternoon nap, he was brought into the living room to open the mountain of gifts he had waiting for him. And wouldn't you know it? Belinda asked me to go first. So, I took my gift over to John who was sitting on Bronwyn's lap (Belinda's sister) and handed it to the pair. As they both unwrapped it, everyone's eyes were fixed on them. The wrapping paper fell away and Bronwyn held up the bear.

"What the hell is this?"

The different reactions from people, as they realised what the present was, were hilarious.

Some were laughing and some had a look of confusion on their faces. In the end, everyone saw the funny side of it. Belinda's grandparents didn't even understand what it was all about so, in the end, no one was offended. Later in the day, when other guests dropped in to say hello, the first gift they were always shown was the bondage teddy.

Recently, for his 16th birthday, I gave John a book of insults. Do you think I'm a bad influence?

Bondage Bob

Lyrics:

It's Christmas 2001
The first Christmas for Neville's son
I bought a gift for baby John
A toy unfit for a boy so young

But my present to John was the best bar none
A surprise to all, designed to stun
A soft toy bear—cuddly and fun
And the fun had just begun.

Bondage Bob
The next heartthrob
Bondage Bob
From the novelty shop
Bondage Bob
He wears a leather top
Bondage Bob
From the novelty shop

You see, I bought a bear in bondage wear
With leather straps and underwear
The parents were there, but they didn't care
And the grandparents, well they were unaware
Bob the bear, super debonair,

His love for handcuffs a real bugbear,
You can't take him anywhere.

Bondage Bob
The next heartthrob
Bondage Bob
From the novelty shop
Bondage Bob
He wears a leather top
Bondage Bob
From the novelty shop

Bridge (tag poem):
"I wear my leather, no matter what the weather.
With whips and chains, I'll please with pain.
Let me ride you with a saddle; let me hit you with a paddle
Stay by my side, I'll keep you satisfied."

Bondage Bob
The next heartthrob
Bondage Bob
From the novelty shop
Bondage Bob
He wears a leather top
Bondage Bob
From the novelty shop

The Horny German Truck Driver

Have you ever been offered sex for money but weren't sure if you had to pay or if the other person was going to pay? Have you ever felt you were unwittingly living out a scene from a German porno film? No and no? Funnily enough, my answers are yes and yes. Both scenarios happened to me in the one incident.

It was July 1997. I was 23 at the time and

backpacking around Germany. I had spent the weekend with my German friend, Julia, and her family in the small village of Bad Breisig, 30km south of Bonn.

It was Monday and I needed to make my way down south to a small village called Kempten, roughly 500km away. I had some English friends there who I'd been staying with and using their flat as a base whilst I was travelling around. With my savings low and being a weekday, the cheapest way to make the trip was to hitchhike. Julia made me a sign in German saying I was an Australian looking for a ride. We hoped the Aussie link would make people stop. Armed with the sign, and a map from Julia's father, they drove me to a rest stop on a nearby motorway where I could start to look for a ride. It's illegal for vehicles to stop on the *autobahn* so to hitch a ride you have to find one at rest stops. There were a few ways to go about getting a ride. One was to approach people and to ask to travel with them, or another was to just stand near the exit of the rest stop and hold up a sign as people drove past, in the hope that they'd stop.

I'd made good progress in the morning and hadn't had to wait very long for a ride each time I was looking. Different friendly people had driven me as far as they were going in my direction and, come lunchtime, I was at a large busy truck stop with petrol station, shops and restaurant. After about half an hour of trying the sign method with no luck, I decided to try the direct approach. With my very limited German, I walked through the car park, asking around.

I noticed a truck drive past and pull up. I saw the driver hop out and I decided to ask him. Instead, he came over to me and asked if I needed a lift. Hell, yeah. I noticed his fly was undone and just thought the idiot had forgotten to do it up when he last went to the toilet. If only that were true.

We were on our way down the *autobahn* and I quickly noticed a porn mag sitting on the dash. The truckie looked at me and said I could have a look if I wanted to. After a few minutes, he asked me if I liked the mag. I smiled and kept looking. Not long later, he asked if it was making my dick hard. WHAT? That's a bit fuckin' personal, I thought. He revealed that looking through the magazine makes his dick hard. He started to rub the bulge in his trousers and it suddenly dawned on me why his fly was undone.

This guy was about 5'72" (I'm talking about his height, not the length of anything!), quite slim, had short brown hair and a porno-star moustache. With him excited and his fly undone, I could see he was wearing bright pink underwear. What was that all about? He said something like, once he's hard he likes to have sex or to wank. Do I need to know this, I thought? He kept saying the word 'mush', whilst miming the wanking motion. I concluded that mush must mean wank. He kept touching himself. I thought he was going to have a wank right there and then, in front of me, as we were motoring down the *autobahn*.

To add to my 'this must be a dream' mindset, he said, "50 Deutsch Mach". I nervously asked what was 50DM? He said a few words, including the word 'mush'. I innocently thought he was saying he pays 50DM to have a wank. I thought, what an idiot; everyone else does it for free. But then he kept mentioning it and I realised it wasn't a statement but a question.

What you must realise is that all this was in German. I was struggling to get my head around the language, as well as the fact I was being propositioned by a male German truck driver. I hid behind the language barrier and pretended not to understand. Not that I had to pretend. The truth was, I didn't understand. 50DM was to pass hands but that's all I knew. Who was to pay who? Who would have to do the mushing to whom? Would there be more than mushing? Oh, fuck! Get me off this truck.

I continued to play dumb, afraid of his reaction if I turned him down. Would he turn violent if I said no? Travelling down the highway at over 100km with nowhere to run and with no control over where the guy was driving me, what could I do? Admittedly, there wasn't a lot he could have done to me whilst driving the truck but, at the same time, I was a passenger, just a long for the ride, totally at the mercy of my chauffeur.

Well, this could have gone on forever—he asking for some sort of sexual favour and me pretending not to understand. Maybe that's what I should have aimed to do until we got to the next rest stop. In the end, I just said no; I wasn't interested.

Expecting the worst, once again, the truckie's behaviour came from left field and surprised me. The guy became all normal. He started asking me if I was studying in Germany or just travelling around. He asked about Australia and other countries I'd been. That didn't stop me from asking to get off at the next stop though, even though the guy was going in my direction a lot farther.

I sat down at the stop for a second to collect my thoughts. I asked myself, "What just happened there?" Unfortunately, I couldn't get the picture of the truck driver touching himself through his pink underwear out of my head.

I later managed to get a lift to the nearby town of Augsburg where I caught a train the rest of the way to Kempten. I arrived in Kempten in the evening and went straight to the pub to meet up with my English mates. I had everyone in stitches telling them about the horny truck driver.

Horny German Truck Driver

Lyrics:

I found myself hitchhikin' on the road in Germany
I had me a sign explaining my next destiny
Just when I thought a ride wasn't meant to be
Along came a trucker who stopped to pick up me

He said, "How do you do? And can I do you too?
I'll have my way with you."
I said, "Not from this land, so I don't understand
Why you don't use your hand."

'Cause he's a
Horny German truck driver
He wants from me a sex favour
It gets lonely on the road
He wants my help to shoot his load
'Cause he's a
Horny German truck driver
Horny German truck driver

He handed me a magazine
which I was keen to read
The naked women in the book,
they were a sight to see
The driver got excited; I could see his pink undies

The next thing I knew he was flirting there with me

He said, "How do you do? And can I do you too?
I'll have my way with you."
I said, "Not from this land, so I don't understand
why you don't use your hand."

'Cause he's a
Horny German truck driver
He wants from me a sex favour
It gets lonely on the road
He wants my help to shoot his load
'Cause he's a
Horny German truck driver
Horny German truck driver

He set the price at 50
Who was to pay, him or me?
I said, "Oh no, I don't agree.
Let me out here," End of story.

Horny German truck driver
Horny German truck driver
He wants from me a sex favour
Horny German truck driver

The Mel & Junior Stand

As a child, when I was lucky enough to go to the local school fair; I always enjoyed going to the face painting stand and having my favourite superhero painted on my face. Fast forward many years to when I was 20 years old and, loitering at the local school oval, I was none too pleased to have paint on my face when paying tribute to one of my football heroes. Unfortunately, I only had myself to blame.

My friends Brian and Derek and I grew up

in the southern suburb of Curtin in Australia's capital city, Canberra. We all went to the same high school together, although we were in different years. Brian was two years ahead of me and Derek one year and we became good friends through catching the same school bus. In the winter months, a group of us on the Curtin school bus organised informal games of footy (tackle or touch rugby league) after school at the south Curtin oval. Brian and I bonded over both of us supporting the Balmain Tigers in the National Rugby League competition. On the occasions that we both arrived early to the game after school, we used to climb onto the roof of the oval toilet block and sit up there looking out over the fields of green below us. Eventually, we named the toilet block 'The Mel & Junior Stand' after our respective favourite Balmain players. Mel was the nickname of my favourite player, David Brooks, and Junior the nickname of Brian's favourite player, Wayne Pearce.

Years after the games of footy had stopped and we'd all left school, there were a couple of times where the three of us returned to the south Curtin oval after a night out on the town. We'd share a cab from a night out in the city centre back to Curtin and spend some time sitting on the oval with a couple of beers and chatting about guy stuff. We were all still living with our parents so we couldn't hang out at someone's house in the early hours of the morning.

I'm sure it was my idea, although I don't remember how it came about, but we thought it would be a good idea to spray-paint the words 'The Mel and Junior Stand' onto the bare, brick wall of the toilet block that faced the oval. So, the next chance we had, we arrived at the oval after a night out, somewhat drunk, and I was armed with a can of black spray-paint I'd been carrying around all night.

There's a quote you might have heard that goes: "When you're in jail, a good friend will be trying to bail you out. A best friend will be in the cell next to you saying, 'Damn, that was fun'." Well, as I made my way across the playing fields towards the toilet block, Derek and Brian disappeared. They wanted nothing to do with the vandalism I was about to commit.

Derek, at the time, was in training to become a police officer so he was definitely going to sit this one out. They both watched from afar, hiding in the shadows of the primary school adjacent to the oval. I guess they'd be bailing me out then, rather than sitting in the cell with me, but I wasn't to be deterred.

It was a dark night, my friends, and the wall in question was also in the shadows. I wasn't wearing my glasses, and this was before the days I wore contact lenses. I took the cap off the spray can bottle. The nozzle was black and a weird shape. I couldn't tell where the hole was for the paint to come out.

I took a guess and pressed down on the nozzle. OH, SHIT! The paint shot out onto my hand. I had the bottle facing the wrong way. The wet, black paint dripped down my hand towards my wrist. I wiped my hand on the grass but that just spread the paint further. Without thinking, I'd scratched an itch on one of my cheeks and then had paint smeared on my face. By this time, I'd lost where the hole was again. I had another attempt at painting the wall but the same thing happened AGAIN.

Jet black paint all over my hand. It was annoying but I wasn't giving up.

On the third attempt, I was able to point the can in the right direction away from me. I held the can in that position and didn't let go so as not to lose the correct spot. Success! I wrote the title in exaggerated uppercase letters, filling the wall with writing. I then headed over to Brian and Derek. They saw the paint on my face and hands, and they both cracked up laughing. I didn't think the situation was as ridiculous as they made it out to be, as it was nothing water and a towel couldn't fix.

We walked five minutes down the road to Curtin shops, where Coles supermarket was open 24 hours. We thought it would be a good idea if I didn't go inside while I had paint all over my hands and face. If anyone came looking for the people responsible for the graffiti, we didn't want witnesses or CCTV footage being able to identify us. I went to the public toilets there and attempted to wash my face and hands as best I could. I managed to wash off most of it but small stubborn patches remained in some parts. We then went back to the south Curtin oval and ate a delectable chocolate Bavarian cake the guys had bought from Coles. After eating the cake, I had chocolate all over my hands and face.

The Mel & Junior Stand

Lyrics:

It's late at night, south Curtin oval,
Me and two mates gonna be antisocial
Wanna cover the toilet block in some graffiti
Got my spray can, should be really easy

But it's really dark as I hold the paint bottle
Can't see where, I'm aiming the nozzle
I point the can at the toilet block
Straightaway, I receive a rude shock

I got paint, paint all over my face
I got paint, paint all over the place
There's more paint, paint on my right hand
Then paint, paint on the Mel and Junior Stand

The nozzle was pointed right at my hand
My hand covered in paint, not what I'd planned
I dropped the can and wiped my face
My cheek smudged with paint, my laughing mates

I got paint, paint all over my face
I got paint, paint all over the place
There's more paint, paint on my right hand
Then paint, paint on the Mel and Junior Stand

I picked up the can to try once more
To paint the bare wall unlike before
I thought I had the aim perfect this time, but then
Can you believe it, I did it again?

I got paint, paint all over my face
I got paint, paint all over the place
There's more paint, paint on my right hand
Then paint, paint on the Mel and Junior Stand

I got paint, paint all over my face
I got paint, paint all over the place
There's more paint, paint on my right hand
Then paint, paint on the Mel and Junior Stand

Brian Oliver

Back in the day, it was common, whilst travelling, to write postcards to your friends and family. It was a bit of a chore though, to be honest. Who could be bothered to take time out of their holiday and think of something to write on the back of a postcard? And who are you going to write to? Everyone wants one. Everyone loves the surprise of finding a postcard in the mailbox. So, who? Your parents? Siblings? Friends? Colleagues from work? What about a complete stranger?

In August of 2002, my mate Crazy Horse and I were in Dublin for the weekend and enjoying a pint in the pub. We'd bought some postcards but had no idea who to write to. We borrowed the Dublin white pages from behind the bar: we opened the book up to a random page, pointed blindly at the list of names, and came up with Brian Oliver.

We, actually, chose four random names: Brian Oliver, William Halpin, Andrew Pye and Thomas Foley. Of the four we chose, Brian Oliver was the only one we wrote more than a few words to. On the other cards, we just drew noughts and crosses games. So, we started writing to Brian as if we were his best friends and had known him for years. We never made anything up. We told the truth about our travels and proceeded to send a postcard from each place we travelled to. But, and here's the best bit, we never revealed our last names or gave a return address and definitely didn't mention he was chosen randomly. We had no way of knowing who we were writing to and this poor confused man was probably wondering why he couldn't remember who these friends of his were.

Months later, Crazy Horse phoned the Oliver household pretending to be from the bank, selling insurance. Brian wasn't home but Crazy spoke to Brian's wife. From the call, we gathered he was in his 50s and we now knew he was married. Knowing that we weren't writing to an old senile man, that was all the encouragement we needed and we told others to write to him as well, when travelling. From what I understood, Brian Oliver quickly racked up a collection of postcards from people he didn't know, from Ireland, the United Kingdom, Spain, Germany, the Czech Republic, Hungary, the United States, Canada, Mexico, South Africa, Hong Kong and Australia. We first started that day in August 2002 and over three years later we were still doing it.

Whilst in Europe for a wedding in October of 2005, I knew I'd be going over to Dublin at some stage to visit a friend from Canberra.

So, I was contemplating the idea of finally meeting up with Brian. I didn't expect to be in that part of the world again anytime soon, so this was maybe my only chance to meet him. Meeting up would answer so many questions that we'd pondered over for years: What's he like? What's his family like, if any? What's his life story? Does he read the cards? What does he think about it all? Does he keep them? Does he share them with his mates down the pub?

Then there was the downside to meeting up. If we were to meet, the joke would be over. No doubt I'd tell him about being chosen randomly to get the answers to our questions but what fun would it be writing another boring old postcard to someone you know?

For three years, I'd become so used to experiencing something and thinking, "I must tell Brian about this," e.g. It was my first thought after a male train attendant made a move on me and grabbed my crotch whilst on a train to Chicago. It's so easy to write to a stranger. You just write as if it's your diary and then make a joke that hints at the fact you've never met, e.g. "I had my head shaved today. You wouldn't recognise me," or "I went out drinking with my mate, Kenny. I don't think you've met Kenny."

After much thought and with a lot of encouragement from friends, I decided to give Brian a call and see what would happen. I rang on the only night I was free to see him and his wife answered the phone. I asked for Brian and was told he was at work and asked if I wanted to leave a message. I asked her could she please let Brian know that his mate, Spaceman, called. After saying that, I was expecting the Spanish Inquisition. "Spaceman? You're that fucker that keeps sending postcards and we don't even know who the fuck you are!" But there was none of that. She took my number and then the call was over.

I later realised I couldn't receive incoming calls on my mobile so I'd have to phone back. I spoke to Mrs Oliver again and found out that Brian would be home at 7pm. After a few more pints in the pub, I phoned at 7:30 and this time Brian answered. "This will be interesting," I thought. Crazy Horse had rung a few times in the past as Abdul Al Halleel, pretending to sell insurance, to try and get some idea of what kind of person Brian was. But here I was ringing, revealing my true identity.

"Hi, is that Brian?"

"Yes."

"Oh, hi. It's Spaceman."

Now, surely, I would get the third degree, but no. Brian asked, "How are you?" as if I was some long-time friend. I explained that I was in town for the night and asked if he wanted to catch up for a pint. We arranged to meet up and he gave me the bus number to Coolock—his part of town—and we arranged to meet at the bus stop where I was to get off. I'd know to get off because the stop was in front of a church.

I was a bit lazy and didn't feel like catching a bus so I caught a cab and asked the driver to take me to Coolock. On the way, he asked me where in Coolock I wanted. "Oh, just in front of the church, please mate."

"But there's a church on every second corner in Dublin."

Not to worry, we worked out which was the correct church and, because I caught a cab, I'd arrived early. I sat at the bus stop waiting for Brian. Unbeknownst to me, he had arrived and was standing behind me, thinking I was someone waiting for the bus. After a while, I noticed a guy standing behind the bus stop. Was this Brian? God, he's older than I thought. Well, let's find out.

I went over and asked, "Are you Brian?"

"Yes."

"Hi, I'm Spaceman."

I put my hand out to shake his. The moment of truth. Face to face with Brian Oliver. A man I knew only by address. The man who, for the last three years and three months, had been bombarded with postcards from all over the world, from people he didn't know, and I had been a major player. Was Brian going to shake my hand or punch me in the face? We shook hands.

"Let's get in out of the cold," he said.

We walked together to the pub a few hundred metres down the road. We made small talk as we went, once again as if we were old friends catching up. Did Brian think that we were, indeed, friends but couldn't remember from where and was too embarrassed to say?

But only minutes earlier, I had to ask him if he was Brian Oliver. Surely, he realised we were meeting for the first time.

We arrived at the pub and Brian got the first round in. We sat at the bar, said cheers and took a sip from our beer. And then it came, the first acknowledgement from Brian of the last three years.

"So," then a brief pause, "what's the story with all the postcards?"

I couldn't help but laugh. After that we both told each other our sides of the story. Brian was a nice guy and appreciated the humour behind the cards. Brian, I'm guessing, was in his fifties, about 5'7", had short dark grey hair, wore glasses and had a grey moustache. He is a Dubliner born and bred. He is married with four grownup sons and works as a computer technician.

Brian explained that, when the first cards started coming, he threw them out thinking we had the wrong person. But when they kept coming, he suspected something was going on and started to keep them all. It was a big thing in the Oliver household when a new card arrived. It was Brian and his youngest son Dave who tried to get to the bottom of it all. They looked for any clues as to how they might track us down.

The closest they came was when our friend, Jane, in Virginia, US, left an address on a card of a riding school she went to. But after tracking down the school phone number, the Oliver lads thought it was a bit absurd to ring up asking for someone called Jane who knows a Spaceman and Crazy Horse. Brian didn't believe we used our real names. Otherwise, if he'd put our names in a Google search he would have found us. We also once let slip that we drank in The Royal Bar, in Belfast, but he never called the pub.

After a few rounds, Brian's son Dave came and joined us. He was a good guy as well and introduced me to Fat Frogs (Blue Wicked, Orange Cruiser and Bacardi Breezer; all mixed together to create a green lemonade tasting drink that goes down so smoothly). Another son, Keith, also dropped in on his way to the theatre and brought with him a pile of postcards. Brian and I counted 120 postcards in just this one pile. Brian said he had more at home and then there were the ones he'd thrown out. I sat there looking through them. I could have sat there for hours reading them but it would have been a bit anti-social. I just glanced through them and saw postcards from people who I had no idea who they were. Crazy Horse and I never made copies of the cards we sent, so it was a good trip down memory lane reading some of them again. We spent the night chatting and getting very drunk. I was on such a high when we called it a night.

All in all, Brian took the whole experience in the good humour in which it was intended. None of the postcards were ever rude or vindictive in any way. So, the joke was over now but I had made a new friend. Well, actually, we'd been friends for years, but now we knew who each other was.

This song is written from the point of view of before I met Brian and is a fun tongue-in-cheek dig at Brian for never writing back. .

Brian Oliver

Lyrics:

Brian Oliver, why don't you write?
Is there something about me
That you don't like?
Brian Oliver, hey man, what gives?
Don't forget, now, I know where you live.

You, me and Crazy Horse we go way back,
We've had our share of some mighty good craic.
On our travels, we always send you mail,
One or two postcards without fail.

Brian Oliver, why don't you write?
Is there something about me
That you don't like?
Brian Oliver, hey man, what gives?
Don't forget, now, I know where you live.

You've always been welcome to join us mate,
But you've never come along, no, not to date.
23 Moatfield, Dublin 5
No word from you to say that you're alive.

Brian Oliver, why don't you write?
Is there something about me

That you don't like?
Brian Oliver, hey man, what gives?
Don't forget, now, I know where you live.

I could always write to Andrew Pye,
Or Thomas Foley, now they're both great guys.
You've turned real cold and you've put up a wall,
I have to say Brian, I don't know you at all.

Brian Oliver, why don't you write?
Is there something about me
That you don't like?
Brian Oliver, hey man, what gives?
Don't forget, now, I know where you live.

Brian Oliver. I know where you live.
Brian Oliver. I know where you live.
Brian Oliver. I know where you live.

Brian Oliver

Did you know you only get ten minutes?

For the milestone of my 30th birthday, I decided to invite some friends to join me on a weekend away. And the location? None other than... Amsterdam. There were ten of us in total and, on the day of my birthday, Monday 3rd May 2004, we all assembled at a café by a canal.

My dear friend, Tessa, gave me quite a unique birthday present. After tearing away the wrapping paper, I discovered I was the proud owner of a new briefcase. But, this was not a business briefcase. This was a small, white, plastic briefcase that contained a T-shirt and loads of individual letters, numbers and symbols that could be stuck onto the front of the shirt with Velcro to make your own messages or slogans. How wicked is that?

I opened the briefcase, still not sure what it was. I found the T-shirt and unfolded it to see the following message already arranged on the front:

"Did you know you only get 10 minutes?" – Spaceman

My friends and I burst out laughing. What a wonderful, thoughtful and topical gift. What did it mean? It was a statement I had made after a disastrous visit to one of the windows in the red-light district that climaxed in an argument with two Dutch women over the duration of our business arrangement and left my mate €80 out of pocket. Unfortunately, there were no other climaxes to speak of.

Let's rewind two days to the Saturday night. We all went out drinking and dancing, found ourselves a cool little bar full of locals and a good time was had by all. Later, after everyone else had called it a night, my mate, Vinnie, and I found ourselves window shopping through the red-light district. As a birthday present, Vinnie offered to treat me to a hooker and we found two sexy blondes in the same window who were Dutch (that may seem obvious seeing as we were in Holland but the majority of sex workers in Amsterdam are from Eastern Europe).

They closed the curtain of their window/door and took us to the back of the room. Inside was a single bed against the wall with a large wall mirror above it. On the opposite side of the room, was a woman who looked to be in her fifties and she was just sitting there, not saying much. I'm guessing she was the pimp. She soon got up and left us to it.

So, we took our clothes off and the two blondes were very businesslike and not too friendly. They weren't exactly creating an erotic environment. The four of us were sharing the single bed and my chick lay on her back and said, "Fuck me big boy," which made me laugh. I thought she could have at least tried to sound like she meant it. We got underway and, by this stage of the night, I was extremely wasted. I didn't have a problem getting it up, I just couldn't come anytime soon.

To add to her unfriendly demeanour, my woman started complaining that I was taking too long. I asked her if she could move a little bit closer as we were in an awkward position.

"NO!" was her quick response.

So, I asked if I could reposition her legs to make things a little easier and once again my request was met with a big "No".

I tried to make the best of the situation but, before I could get into a rhythm, she told me to stop because time was up. I was like, "What the fuck? We've not long started." She said that you only get 10 minutes. Once she said that, well, we had a huge argument, which wasn't creating the best environment for Vinnie and his woman. I was shouting, "I haven't finished yet. I didn't know you only get 10 minutes." I'd always found the women I'd been with to be really happy if I lasted longer than 10 minutes. Now, this chick was telling me I was taking too long. Plus, I didn't think ten minutes had gone by, anyway.

She argued, "Everyone knows you only get 10 minutes. There's a sign on the door."

I stormed out to the street and asked the first person I saw, "Did you know you only get 10 minutes?"

The man answered, "No."

I stormed back into the room, "See. Not everyone knows you only get 10 fuckin' minutes."

She became moralistic, "Don't swear in here."

This is after, mind you, she had earlier said, "Fuck me, big boy."

Well, all of this ruined it for Vinnie. His chick stopped as well, before they even really got started. We were both told to leave or they'd get their pimp. We laughed as we didn't think a woman in her fifties would pose much of a threat. We told them to go get their pimp but they both stayed put in the room.

Vinnie tried to appeal to their compassionate side and explained that it was my birthday, but I don't think these women had a soft side.

I mean ... where's the love? Hahaha. I thought they were in the wrong line of work. I thought they would have made better dominatrices than 'love providers'. So, anyway, Vinnie and I got dressed and left.

Whilst out sightseeing the next day, I told all my friends about the drama with the hookers the night before. They all thought it was hilarious. So, on Monday, after receiving my amusing birthday present from Tessa, I wore the shirt immediately. Partly as a tongue-in-cheek community announcement as I wanted everyone to know that the women behind the windows are all about wham, bam, thank you ma'am.

Did you know you only get ten minutes?

Lyrics:

I'm window shopping and I'm in Amsterdam
The perfect place for wham, bam,
thank you ma'am
It's my birthday and it's my mate's treat
We make our way to the red-light streets

We find a window with two Dutch blondes
We pay the pimp and then off she's gone
A single bed and a party of four
We try to make love but they make war

"Time's up; you only get ten minutes."
"What the fuck? We're not yet close to finished."
"Sorry boys, you only get ten minutes."

"I didn't know you only get ten minutes
When with a girl I always try to finish
A lot longer than just ten minutes."

My woman says that everyone knows
About the time-limit without clothes
I'm near the door so I ask someone there
They shake their head. They had no idea

The fun now stops for my friend, too
Stopped early, before he was through
A single bed and a party of four
We tried to make love but they made war

"Time's up; you only get ten minutes."
"What the fuck? We're not yet close to finished."
"Sorry boys, you only get ten minutes."

"I didn't know you only get ten minutes
When with a girl I always try to finish
A lot longer than just ten minutes."

"I didn't know you only get ten minutes
When with a girl I always try to finish
A lot longer than just ten minutes."

It's on FIRE!

When you think of embarrassing moments in your life, which ones still make you cringe all these years later? For me, having two firetrucks rock up to an inner-city park because I nearly caused an explosion, is up there as one of my most embarrassing moments. Thankfully, I can laugh about it now.

In November 1999, my girlfriend at the time and I packed our Toyota Hiace van full of camping equipment ready for our next adventure. Manny was a lovely French woman. We met through mutual friends in London 18 months earlier. We both liked to travel and had taken many trips together. This trip, however, was an adventure into the unknown. With no set timeframe, we went exploring along the NSW south coast in our mobile home and over the border into Victoria, stopping finally in Melbourne.

We were still there, four weeks later, enjoying the culture and living out of our van. We had a little gas burner, which we used to boil water with so we could cook noodles, or heat up canned foods and have coffee. The gas bottle was from the 70s; I had commandeered it out of my mother's belongings in the garage. So, one day when it ran out of gas, we had to buy a new bottle because no one would refill our ancient bottle due to it being too old. In the end, we spent $50 on a new bottle, plus we had to buy an extra attachment so our stove top would fit.

Later that day, we pulled up at an inner-city park (Carlton Gardens for those of you who know Melbourne) to boil water for some coffee. This was the first time we'd used the new gas bottle since buying it. And wouldn't you know it, the fuckin' gas bottle caught on fire. The new attachment we'd bought connected the bottle to the stove top. It had two outlets and the one we weren't using mustn't have been closed properly and was therefore leaking gas. Actually, I don't know why the fuck it caught on fire, except for the obvious reason ... I put a match to it.

All I knew was that I had a burning gas bottle in the back of our van with flames about 30cm high. I wanted the gas bottle out of the van as quickly as possible. I picked the bottle up and put it out onto the footpath. What I failed to notice was that the footpath had a slant. Whilst I was looking in the van for water, the gas bottle, which by now had some angry, loud, roaring flames erupting from it, fell over... and rolled under the van.

PANIC!

I thought the whole fuckin' van might blow up. I knew I had to move the van but I didn't want to start it in case there was a spark that set the whole thing off. I quickly ran to the driver's door and put the van into neutral, then pushed it down the hill away from the flamin' danger.

I threw what little amount of water I had on the gas bottle but it just kept burning. We couldn't turn the gas off, as the fire was too large and too hot to put our hands near. My arm hairs got singed trying. We tried to smother the flames with a towel but they were too strong. The bottle just lay in the gutter, burning so fiercely and at a scary loud volume.

Meanwhile, this old hippie passing by started to give us a ten-minute lecture on the safeties of camping. "Too fuckin' late," I thought. He had no advice as what to do about an out of control gas bottle.

We couldn't just get out the marshmallows and sit around the fire waiting for the gas to burn out. It was new and had ten hours' worth of gas left in it. I thought it was time to call the fire superheroes. We had just bought a new mobile phone but I hadn't worked out how to use it yet. So, here I was walking around with a phone in my hand, yet asking passers-by if they had a phone. I felt like I was walking around with my dick in my hand the way people were looking at me.

In the end, I threw one of our blankets on the fire to smother the gas bottle. Flames started to shoot out from under the blanket at my legs. That was fun (sarcasm). But I fought back and completely choked it of oxygen and the fire died.

"Die you fucker," I yelled.

I yelled as if I had just stuck a knife into a voodoo doll. Actually, I don't think I yelled that at all, but that's how I felt.

The fire was out and I sat down with black ash over my hands and wiped my sweaty brow in time to see two big, firetrucks coming down the street to make the whole matter even more embarrassing. I thought we were going to be in trouble but the firefighters were just concerned that we were alright and were curious as to what had happened. They suggested we go to the café around the corner and buy a coffee next time.

Well, we lost $50 but we could have lost our van or even ourselves. All of this happened in a little park in the city, about 2 mins from the

CBD. It's hard to explain in words how fuckin' scared I was when all this was going on. It didn't help when I saw the fear in Manny's eyes. It only took a couple of paragraphs to tell the story but the whole incident from start to finish was a long 25 minutes.

We bought a new gas bottle… again. Every time I went to light it and the sudden burst of flames occurred, like when you're lighting a gas grill or oven, I jumped back and my heart would miss a beat. One morning, a week or two later, when I was leaving work, the radio in the van caught on fire. But that's another story.

Radio on fire story

The second verse of the song is about this little anecdote. During our time in Melbourne, I was working nightshift at a plastics factory. One morning, when I'd finished for the night, I hopped in my van and started 'her' up. I turned my head around to see if all was clear as I reversed out. When I turned my head around to face the front again the whole fuckin' cabin was full of smoke. I couldn't see a thing. Oh, great, another fuckin' fire in the van. Except this time, it was the van itself. Well, shit! In Hollywood, cars blow up really easily so I flew into panic mode. I didn't want the van blowing up because losing the van would just suck. But, also, because I was living out of it at the time, it was my home. Oh yeah, and I almost forgot—the most important reason—my girlfriend Manny was fast asleep in the back.

I turned the engine off and quickly ran around to the sliding door to see if I could find something to put the fire out with. I shouted to Manny "Wake up!!! There's a fire in the van." There was no chance she was getting, "Morning, rise and shine." Or "Hi honey, I've made you breakfast in bed." I can only imagine what it would be like to be woken up with someone shouting, "Fire".

There was another guy in the car park, sitting in his car, getting a few more minutes sleep before he started his shift. He told me later, he'd opened his eyes to see my van full of smoke and he wasn't sure if he was dreaming or not.

Well, Manny's not really a morning person and she stayed in bed. Probably still half asleep and not aware of what was going on. I returned to the driver's side to see the smoke clearing. It was then that I could see what was burning. The fuckin' radio decided it was going to take up smoking. The wires for the radio weren't connected but were still live. They'd come loose and were touching metal. So, when I started up the van, they started burning and burnt themselves out after a few seconds. So, there was no real danger, no real need to panic and, in the end, I didn't have a good excuse for not making Manny breakfast in bed. I guess we weren't in Hollywood.

It's on FIRE!

Lyrics:

Driving in our van
Camping where we can
Driving with an open throttle
Cooking with our dodgy gas bottle
Stop for a well-earned break
Want some coffee, yeah, thanks mate
Stand back I'm lighting the gas
Oh fuck, shit man, move your arse

It's on FIRE!!

There's a fire in the van
Thank God we're not in Hollywood
Can't find the water can
So glad we're not in Hollywood
The explosion would be grand
If this scene were made it Hollywood
Gonna call the fireman
He'll save the day like no one could.

Hopping in the van
Gonna take off once again
Turn the key and the engine starts
Gonna reverse right out of this carpark

I turn and it ain't no joke
The cabin's full of thick smoke

It's on FIRE!!

There's a fire in the van
Thank God we're not in Hollywood
Can't find the water can
So glad we're not in Hollywood
The explosion would be grand
If this scene were made it Hollywood
Gonna call the fireman
He'll save the day like no one could.

Sweet Derrière

How funny is it watching those Olympic race walkers? The technique, involving such pronounced hip movements, looks quite ridiculous. Although, having said that, there is a lot of skill involved in race walking. I read that, with the correct technique, race walkers can walk a mile faster than the average person can run. It's the kind of walk I'd do if I were to mimic a funny walk—arms pumping, butt swaying and a scrunched-up face mimicking extreme discomfort. But it was far from funny when, one day, I was forced to stride like a race walker due to a mindless error in a fire-breathing display. The look of pain on my face, due to what felt like barbed-wire up my arse, was 100% genuine in this instance. There was no mimicking whatsoever.

Central London was the location for this blunder. I was out on the town with two mates, bar hopping, in late 1997. We were passing through Leicester Square and we stopped to have a look at some of the street performers. There were two guys performing fire breathing tricks. From memory, I think my mate Barry dared me to have a go. Either way, I went up and put some fuel in my mouth. I held the flaming torch close to my mouth; I opened my mouth ... and nothing. Whoops! I didn't know you weren't meant to swallow the fuel. Oh man, what a blunder. That was definitely going to come back and bite me on the bum.

I did it again. This time I kept the fuel in my mouth and breathed over the open flame and ... WHOOSHKA! A big burst of fire shot out from the torch like a fireball. That was the intended result and what should have happened the first time. We left and went to another pub.

It wasn't long before I developed an extremely sore throat and, no matter what I drank, I couldn't get rid of it. I even tried drinking milk, which I don't like, but that didn't help either. In the end, I decided just to get really pissed on Southern Comfort in the hoep that being drunk would relieve the soreness.

When I woke the next morning, OH ... MY ... GOD! It felt like I had a multitude of razor blades jammed up my arse. I had an extremely sharp, piercing pain in the rectum as the fuel was being expelled from my body. I could feel the streams of gas coming out. If someone were to have lit a match near my arse, I would have had great balls of fire. Moving around was very painful and only possible at a snail's pace. The pain only lasted that one day and, thankfully, I had the day off work. However, I wasn't able to lay idle at home. I remember having to go to the bank on High Street Kensington and walking in slow motion with the hip movements of an Olympic racer and extreme facial contortions too. That was *not* an enjoyable experience.

You probably won't be surprised to hear that I've never made the mistake of swallowing fuel again.

Sweet Derrière

Lyrics:

A word of advice when fire breathing
Be sure not to swallow the fuel
What happened to me, could happen to you,
Oh man, I was such a fool

I held the flame out in front of my face
And I opened my mouth there in Leicester Square
But there was no combustion,
I'd swallowed the paraffin
Oh, my poor sweet derrière

Wooooh, my sweet derrière
The pain is more,
More than I can bear.
Woooo-wo-oh, my sweet derrière
The pain is more,
More than I can bear.

And I'm striding like an Olympic walker
I'm moving in slow motion
There's gas coming out of my ass
And I'm hoping there's no explosion

The pain is written on my face
Feels like a thorn bush jammed
up you know where
With every step there's a sharp pain
Oh, my poor sweet derrière

Wooooh, my sweet derrière
The pain is more,
More than I can bear.
Woooo-wo-oh, my sweet derrière
The pain is more,
More than I can bear.

Oooooo, my sweet derrière
It's the worst for wear
Oooooo, my sweet derrière
I hope it can be repaired

And I'm striding like an Olympic walker
I'm moving in slow motion
There's gas coming out of my ass
And I'm hoping there's no explosion

The pain is written on my face
Feels like a thorn bush jammed
up you know where
With every step there's a sharp pain
Oh, my poor sweet derrière

Wooooh, my sweet derrière
(Oh, yeah)
The pain is more,
(The pain is more)
More than I can bear.
Woooo-wo-oh, my sweet derrière
(Oh, yeah)
The pain is more,
(The pain is more)
More than I can bear.

Woooo-wo-oh, my sweet derrière
My sweet derrière
My sweet derrière

I don't like Cricket

This song is not on the CD. You can listen to it at my YouTube channel. Google Spaceman Africa the Musical YouTube channel and you can listen to this and many other songs there. Subscribe to my channel whilst you're there, as well, to receive notifications of new music and videos.

In 1997, when I was backpacking around Germany, there was a train ticket called the *Wochenende* ticket. It was a ticket valid only on weekends for unlimited travel on the regional trains throughout the whole country. The beauty of this ticket was that, for just 35DM (about €18), up to five people could travel on this one ticket. This brought about the practice of travellers hopping onto the train ticketless, searching for someone with a *Wochenende* ticket and asking to travel with them and thus travelling for free. When the ticket collector came around, they simply said they were travelling together.

It was generally the tourists that bought the tickets and the locals who travelled for free. I certainly made the most of this ticket whilst I was in Germany. I travelled a lot of kilometres and visited many beautiful places. A variation of the ticket exists today. It now costs €40 for one passenger and €4 for any additional passengers with a limit of five passengers in total.

The other positive to sharing the Wochenende ticket was meeting other people. I met all manner of fellow travellers and locals. The most significant encounter was when I was travelling from Hanover to Hamburg.

At Osnabruck, a Pakistani man boarded the train and asked me if he could ride with me on my *Wochenende* ticket. I said, "Sure." We chatted a little. I learnt that his name was Jamal. He picked up from my bad German that I wasn't a native. When I told him I was from Australia, that was it, I had set him off; he wouldn't shut up about cricket after that.

It was getting close to midnight as we were nearing Hamburg station and Jamal asked where I was staying. I told him I had nothing organised, so planned to sleep at the station and find somewhere in the morning. He said the station was dangerous at night and full of drug addicts. He suggested I stay with him in his flat for the night and he'd show me the next day where a youth hostel was. However, come the next day, he said, "Ah forget it. You can stay here."

It was great staying with Jamal. Jamal was about 34 at the time. Originally born in Pakistan, he'd been living in Germany for 15 years. He lived on the 13th floor of a block of flats, overlooking the *Grindelberg* avenue, and from the lounge room there was a great view over the city. There was a great view of Hamburg's telecommunications tower. We were up just as high.

Although unemployed, Jamal was a chef by trade and cooked some great curries whilst I stayed with him. He showed me around the city and he helped me with my German. He showed a great sense of humour and everything was translated into cricket terminology, e.g. when we had run to catch the bus, he'd call out, "Quick single."

Jamal was also captain/coach of the Hamburg cricket side. It wasn't long before he took me to a training session. The team was mainly made up of ex-pats from the sub-continent. I had been a champion backyard cricket player when I was young but this was the real deal. I was playing with the big boys.

I didn't want to interfere with their training so I started by fielding in the outfield. This is when the fun started. Perhaps I was too far away from the action, because I couldn't see the fuckin' ball. My glasses had been stolen a week earlier when I was in Amsterdam and this was way before I had started wearing contact lenses. So, quite often, the ball would be hit in my direction and would fly straight past me before I even knew it was coming. The others, not knowing of my blindness, thought I was some sort of retard with the way I stood motionless whilst the ball whistled straight past me.

I got bored of all this and sat down in a chair ... in the outfield. I'd given up all hope of stopping the ball and resigned myself to the fact that I was basically just playing fetch. Cricket is like a religion to people from the sub-continent and they take it very seriously. My behaviour didn't go down well with the other players. They spoke to each other in their native tongue and I could sense they were talking about me. Jamal later told me they were saying, "Look at this guy. Has he no respect for the game?"

They asked Jamal, "Where did you find this guy?"

He was like, "I just met him on the train."

Despite my 'lack of respect' for the game, Jamal and I remained friends.

I don't like Cricket

Lyrics:

Jamal captained the Hamburg team
So I went to their training, too.
A real professional team at work
I got to observe what they do.

The team were ex-pats from India
Pakistan and Sri Lanka
They were playing and training
And smelt of coriander

And they say,
"We don't like cricket, oh no
We love it."
"We don't like cricket, oh no
We love it."

We're from different worlds
I'm gonna show some respect
I'll stand in the outfield
Out of your way, don't fret

I stood and waited for a big hit
But it was hard for me to see
My glasses stolen just days before

I was as useful as a dead gumtree

The balls came flying, right past me
Much to my despair
Sick of running, and chasing
So I got myself a chair

And I say,
"I don't like cricket, oh no
It's so shit."
"I don't like cricket, oh no
It's so shit."

We're from different worlds
They said I have no respect
They gave me dirty looks
Like I had some weird defect

And I say,
"I don't like cricket, oh no
It's so shit."
"I don't like cricket, oh no
It's so shit."

The Cat's Mole

Aka: It's a long way to the top (if you're rubbing kitty's mole)

This song is not on the CD. You can listen to it at my YouTube channel. Google Spaceman Africa the Musical YouTube channel and you can listen to this and many other songs there. Subscribe to my channel whilst you're there, as well, to receive notifications of new music and videos.

It's the year 2009 and I'm talking to my good friend, Celia. We were talking about different medical issues, or something like that—I can't remember exactly and Celia suddenly remembers this story. She tells me about a guy she knows who had a pet cat. The guy was playing with the cat one day and noticed an unusual mole on the cat's body. A mole as in a spot or blemish on the skin, usually dark in colour and slightly elevated.

The guy was curious as to whether the mole was painful for the cat. He rubbed the mole and, rather than be in pain, the cat seemed to really enjoy having the mole rubbed. So, from then on, the guy rubbed the mole regularly to make his cat happy.

Sometime later, for an unrelated reason, the man took his cat to the vet. Whilst he had the opportunity, he thought he'd ask the vet about the mole, just to make sure there was nothing to worry about.

The vet exclaimed, "Mole? That's not a mole."

So, Celia's telling me this story and at this stage I'm thinking, "Oh my god. It's cancer. The poor cat has cancer."

Luckily, I was sitting down. I wasn't expecting

what came next. So, Celia continues the story:

"Mole? That's not a mole. That's the cat's penis."

Oh my god. I nearly wet myself laughing. To think he was rubbing the cat's penis all that time.

Celia later suggested it would be a good story to write a song about, so I set about trying to come up with something. In the end, I borrowed the AC/DC song *It's a long way to the top*, and just changed the lyrics to match the story. I had a friend record me playing the song and I put it on YouTube. When I told Celia about the song and she heard it, she thought it was hilarious. She told her whole family about it. I believe the guy in the story has even heard the song too.

The Cat's Mole

Lyrics:

Resting from a long day
Going with the flow
Kitty's coming my way
Showing off his mole

Getting felt up, and he moans
Puts his feet up, and he groans
Rub it soft, rub it rough
I tell you folks, my cat can't get enough

I swear I'm not gay, what a shock,
it's a penis not a mole
What a sad day, had to stop rubbing
little kitty's mole
You think it's easy here from where I stand?
Today, no one will shake my hand
What can I say, it's a cock and I thought
it was a mole

Getting felt up, and he moans
Puts his feet up, and he groans
Rub it soft, rub it rough
I tell you folks, my cat can't get enough

Is it OK, Doc, if I'm rubbing kitty's mole
You say it's foul play, what a croc,
no more touching kitty's pole
You think it's easy now that I've been banned,
From touching cats in my homeland?
What can I say, it's a cock and I thought
it was a mole

What can I say, it's a cock
and I thought
it was a mole
I swear I'm not gay, what a shock,
it's a penis
not a mole
What can I say, it's a cock and
I thought it was a mole

Whiteboard Rafting

This song is not on the CD. You can listen to it at my YouTube channel. Google Spaceman Africa the Musical YouTube channel and you can listen to this and many other songs there. Subscribe to my channel whilst you're there, as well, to receive notifications of new music and videos.

"Let go! Let go!" pleaded Elise.

With some reluctance, I shoved Elise, sending her down the steep, slippery street on an imitation toboggan. Elise slid fast over the cobblestones towards the intersection at the bottom of the hill. I watched on with apprehension. It wasn't possible to see if any traffic was going to pass through the intersection below when Elise arrived. There was no conventional way for her to stop her makeshift chariot either, i.e. no brakes. Had I just pushed Elise to her doom? Was her life about to flash before her eyes? How was I going to explain this to the cops?

The night had started in a safe manner in the Peruvian city of Cusco in April, 2012. I was hanging out in Cusco for a month whilst roaming around South America. You might know Cusco as being the gateway to the ancient Inka city—Machu Picchu. In my time there, I met some weird and wonderful people, including Elise—a lovely, vivacious woman from England. We hit it off from the moment we met and spent a lot of time hanging out together. Due to living many years in the UK, I could relate easily to Elise and understand any cultural references she used from her home country. We were both left speechless, one day, when sitting in the Crown Bar and chatting about life.

"I went to Brazil for a rave," revealed Elise.

I knew a female DJ that I used to work with in London, back in the late 90s, who I knew had played at a lot of festivals in Brazil. Just on the off chance I asked:

"Do you know Sally Doolally?"

"Yeah," Elise looked at me weirdly.

"Yeah, so do I," I added.

"Do you know Michael Wilkie?" Elise asked tentatively, as if the answer might be scary.

"Yeah, I know him."

Michael, or Wilkie, as everyone called him, was Sally's boyfriend back in the late 90s. I knew him through Sally and bumped into him every now and then at parties. I knew Sally and Wilkie had broken up a long, long time ago but I wasn't ready for the bombshell that dropped from Elise's mouth.

"I used to go out with him. We were together for four years."

I looked at Elise in total shock—partly in a 'Wow, I can't believe it. What a small world' kind of way. And partly in a 'I can't believe you went out with *him*' kind of way. I was blown away that a mature and cultured woman such as Elise would go out with Wilkie. To be honest, I'd always thought of Wilkie as a bit of a clown. But that was another time, in another life. Maybe he'd changed since I knew him. We all grow and change as the years pass by. Elise was blown away, as well. We sat shaking our heads in disbelief for the next hour.

Anyway, all of this has very little to do with the story behind Whiteboard Rafting. So, one evening, I went to a trivia night at The Muse—a bar/restaurant/nightclub—close to Cusco's main square. The trivia quiz was being hosted by the South American Explorers' Club (SAE).

Elise was an employee of the club and was one of two people running the show. As the quiz progressed, the scores of the different competing teams were written up on a whiteboard brought by the SAE staff from their clubhouse.

After many challenging questions, the quiz came to an end. Who knew it's possible to lead a cow upstairs but not downstairs? Anyway, Elise and I met up after the quiz to continue with the night's frivolities. Because Elise was living at the SAE clubhouse, she was lumped with the job of having to take the whiteboard back. No worries. We thought we'd take the board back and then head out again. I'd given up the booze a few years earlier so I was completely sober but Elise was rather drunk by this stage. So, it was no surprise that she was keen to stop in at a reggae bar we passed along the way for a drink or two. It's not every day a Brit, an Australian and a whiteboard walk into a bar. It wasn't a problem; we just lent the whiteboard up against a wall whilst we had a few refreshments.

When we finally left, it was around 10pm and the narrow streets were quite empty. We got to the base of *Cuesta San Blas* on *Choquechaca Street*. *Cuesta San Blas* is a steep narrow cobblestone street which we had to climb to get back to the SAE clubhouse. The cobblestones at times can be very slippery. To say we struggled walking up the hill, with one of us drunk, and both of us trying to hold a whiteboard, is an understatement. We were slipping all over the place. About halfway into the ascent, 30 metres up from the base of the hill, all this slipping and sliding gave me an idea.

"Hey, why don't we slide down the hill on the whiteboard?"

And to think I was the sober one. One would have expected such a suggestion from the drunk person. Elise didn't need any persuading. She had the whiteboard positioned flat, in the middle of the street, in a flash. She quickly sat down on the board and had her legs crossed ready to take the whiteboard for a test drive. She moved her weight back and forth in an attempt to get the board moving.

"Give me a push."

I put my hands on Elise's back and started

to move her forward. Just as the board was about to take off down the slope, I had second thoughts. What if a car came along at the bottom of the hill? I quickly grabbed the edge of the board, stopping it from moving any further. I didn't want Elise to hurt herself.

"Let go! Let go!" she pleaded.

Oh, what the hell, I thought. I let go and gave her a big shove to help her on her way. She slid down the street, cheering as she went. I'm quite confident in saying that she was the first person to slide down *Cuesta San Blas* on a whiteboard. And at the time I thought maybe the first person to get killed doing it. *Oh shit. What have I done?* I watched on, holding my breath, hoping that everything would be OK. My anxiety turned to amusement when the whiteboard got caught on a cobblestone, stopping dead in its tracks about ten metres short of the intersection. Elise, however, kept going. She fell off the board and rolled down the hill another few metres. I ran down to see if she was alright. I arrived to find she was laughing just as hard as I was. She was fine.

"The Russian judge gives you a ten," I declared.

The board was returned to the clubhouse and a few days later someone noticed that one side of the board was all scratched up.

"What happened here?"

Elise pretended not to hear the question. We laughed about the incident for days afterwards. I coined it a new sport—whiteboard rafting; a play on white water rafting.

I returned to Cusco a few years later with the intention of buying a whiteboard and having a go for myself, riding down *Cuesta San Blas*. I was even hoping to get some video or photos of the event but it never happened. I ended up becoming ill and spending two nights in hospital with bronchitis. Now, there's an idea—ride a hospital bed down *Cuesta San Blas*. Maybe next time.

Whiteboard Rafting

Lyrics:

Whiteboard raftin', everybody's laughin',
It's a whiteboard raftin'.
Whiteboard raftin', it may sound daft, man,
But it's whiteboard raftin'.
Whiteboard raftin', everybody's laughin',
It's a whiteboard raftin'.
Whiteboard raftin', the best pleasure craft, man,
It's a whiteboard raftin'.

Ridin' down *Cuesta San Blas*
Slidin' down, going real fast
Ridin' down *Cuesta San Blas*
Hopin' no traffic comes past

Whiteboard raftin', everybody's laughin',
It's a whiteboard raftin'.
Whiteboard raftin', more skin graftin',
It's a whiteboard raftin'.
Whiteboard raftin', everybody's laughin',
It's a whiteboard raftin'. Woohoohoo
Whiteboard raftin', it ain't no hovercraft, man,
It's a whiteboard raftin'.

Ridin' down *Cuesta San Blas*
Slidin' down, going real fast
Ridin' down *Cuesta San Blas*
Hopin' no traffic comes past

New Orleans Merry-go-round

This song is not on the CD. You can listen to it at my YouTube channel. Google Spaceman Africa the Musical YouTube channel and you can listen to this and many other songs there. Subscribe to my channel whilst you're there, as well, to receive notifications of new music and videos. J

New Orleans was quite the bender. I was stuck in a vicious cycle of late nights, boozing and drunkenness, and I wasn't sure how I was going to escape. Escape was made harder, too, by the fact I'd made so many friends. I met some ultra-friendly people in some of the bars, and some cool and interesting people who drank on the street, your homeless/squatter types. From a proposition to have sex in a church through to meeting a Lucy Lawless lookalike, my time in New Orleans was never dull.

I flew in to New Orleans in May of 2002. I got an airport shuttle van into the city that was to drop all the passengers off at their respective hotels. After a half hour drive, the van pulled into the driveway of an old, weathered, double-storied town-house. It was about 10:30 at night; the house was dimly lit and looked derelict.

"I hope this isn't my stop," I thought.

The driver looked at me and said, "This is you, isn't it?"

"I don't know."

"India House!"

"Yeah, that's me."

I'd booked this place over the phone and was embarrassed to be first drop and at a place that was none too classy. As I was collecting my bags, I felt like saying to the dapper passengers, "My other hotel is the Hyatt."

Anyway, it didn't matter. India House was a good hostel; it had a swimming pool and check-out was at 1pm, which I thought was very civilised. Not that I spent much time there, though. I spent most of my time out and about and used the hostel as a place to sleep and keep my bags.

I found a unique and interesting bar in the French Quarter. I quickly became friends with all the bar staff there and often got cheap/free drinks. It was called Marie Laveau's Voodoo Bar, named after the voodoo queen, Marie Laveau, who was prominent in New Orleans in the 1800s. The bar was only the size of a main bedroom and considerably easy to walk straight past if you didn't know it was there. It's even harder to find nowadays as, unfortunately, it's closed down.

New Orleans has a voodoo and ghost history, and Marie Laveau Voodoo Bar sold real voodoo dolls and spell books. One barmaid, Candice—tall, blonde, mid-30s—worked the day shift and gave me an education in music. She played all this funky 60s and 70s blues music which I loved. She often gave me free drinks and she could make a great Long Island Ice Tea, as well. The other barmaids were friendly, too, but I always tried to go when Candice was working—for the music and the drinks.

Lara was another barmaid. She was an attractive, young brunette, almost Gothic in appearance. She was extremely friendly and good with people. I saw her subdue a group of rowdy men one day, which a less assured woman would have cowered to. I couldn't go all the way to New Orleans and not have a drink of my favoured Southern Comfort. Lara was always happy to serve me the Grand Ol' Drink of the South and even had one with me when I was leaving town.

Early on in my daily pilgrimages to Marie Laveau, I went in one morning and the place was empty, except for the barmaid who was chatting away with a female friend. I hadn't met this barmaid yet; I can't remember her name, but she looked like Lucy Lawless—the

New Zealand actress who played Xena, the Warrior Princess. I sat at the bar and ordered a beer. My hands were shaking big time from an excessive drinking session the night before, and I struggled to hold the beer, which was in a flimsy plastic cup. I asked Lucy Lawless if she could give me a straw. She very kindly obliged, but I could tell I was creeping out her and her friend. So, when I finished the drink, I left so the two could feel at ease. I returned later in the afternoon after I'd had many more drinks and my shakes were a lot calmer. This time, Lara was working.

She asked me, "Were you in here earlier?"
"Yeah."
"Did you drink your beer with a straw?"
"Yeah," I said with a cheeky grin.
"I thought it was you."

Lucy Lawless had told Lara, "Some weird guy came in, shaking like a leaf, and asked for a straw to drink his beer."

I met a young woman, called Willow, who was staying at the same hostel as I was. I was warned by some guys that knew her that she was a bit of a fruit loop, but normally, I'm attracted to people who are a bit different. She was a fruit loop, even for my standards, but that didn't stop me from hanging out with her for three days.

She was short and had fair hair and was somewhat depressive but had a great smile on the occasions I managed to make her laugh. She was from the US, drifting around the country from place to place. She took me to a squat she used to stay at that was supposedly haunted. We borrowed (took) a candle from a Goth bar, and we went to the squat. We'd been there for 10 seconds when, for no apparent reason, the wick fell through the bottom of the candle and landed on the floor. That was a bit freaky. Willow said it had happened to her once before in that house. Without the candle, we were reliant upon her lighter, which got extremely hot and was difficult to hold. I wasn't too comfortable hanging out there without being able to see, so after a brief guided tour, we left.

Earlier that day, we had been hanging out in a park, chatting about life, and Willow asked if I would have sex with her in a church. I said,

"Amen Sister," but even with all the churches in New Orleans, we had trouble finding one open. We decided to go to the French Quarter in search of a church. We walked past a Government office block and Willow said, "Let's use the restroom in here." Unfortunately, security wouldn't let us in and they suggested we use the restroom at McDonalds a few blocks down. No thanks. Not for what we had in mind.

We never did find a church. We became busy looking at haunted houses and touring the streets. I wasn't too upset. I thought we'd be able to find a church the next day, but come the next day, she was on another planet and kept going on about how she had renounced Jesus. We were meant to go bike riding that day, but she said she just wanted to be left alone, so I went into town to Marie Laveau, and I never saw her again. Shame. I quite liked her.

At night in Jackson Square, there were a lot of tarot card readers, palm readers, and psychic stuff like that. Just for a laugh, I decided to have a tarot reading, except, I spoke the whole time in an Irish accent and told the guy I was from Belfast. He asked if I had any questions about my life that he might be able to answer. I asked all these questions about family members that don't exist. Apparently, my older sister (I don't have an older sister) will finally become pregnant and will have a healthy boy. My wife (I'm not married) will leave her current job and find another job quite quickly; there, she will find her calling in life, which will make her happy. I tried my best not to laugh through the reading. I must have been pretty convincing because, whenever I saw him again on the street after that, he always called me the crazy Irish man and I always had to put on the Irish accent again.

Noticing my funds were almost dry, I decided I had to escape the viscous cycle of waking in the afternoon, feeling like shit, drinking for a few hours to feel normal again and, by then, it's too late to organise to travel anywhere, so I stay and drink until the wee hours of the morning. And the cycle starts again. I rang my friend, Monica, in DC and told her I could be on her doorstep very soon as I needed somewhere to stay, quickly. She said it wasn't a problem, and in the meantime, she organised for me to meet up with a friend of hers who lived in New Orleans.

I met up with her friend, Rebecca, in a bar, and she brought along a whole lot of friends too, all girls. I think Rebecca had enticed her friends to come out by saying she was going to meet an Australian guy. Unfortunately for them, I don't fit the Australian stereotype, but we all got along famously, anyway. One of the girls, Janie, invited me to stay at her place for a few days until her parents came to visit. Nice one.

I moved out of the hostel and into a grand house with my own room, which gave me a chance to break my daily routine and sort out my travel plans. With Janie's parents coming to visit in a few days time, there was the added pressure not to procrastinate. After much searching for cheap airfares and rental cars, the decision was to catch a Greyhound bus to DC in a few days.

In the meantime, I hung out with Janie. Janie was a brunette in her late 20s and spoke with a comforting southern accent. We went with some of her friends to a few bars in her area that I hadn't been to before. It was great to see a new part of town. I asked Janie what ward this area was. She said the 7th, and whatever I do, don't go to the 9th; it's dangerous. Woops, too late. Willow and I had wandered through the 9th a few nights earlier.

We stayed up most nights just chatting about things. One night, we didn't stop until 10 in the morning. I was up again a few hours later, off to a bar, where I'd heard there was going to be some good slide guitar on show. That was definitely one good thing about Bourbon Street—the music. The bars were touristy, but you could walk along, and from one bar to the next, there would be a band playing, and if you liked what you heard, you could go in and have a listen for a while. This is the home of Jazz, and I saw quite a lot of good music that was worthy of being on the world stage but was probably only well-known in New Orleans.

After 10 days in 'The Big Easy', I was on my way. I was absolutely grateful to Janie. If she hadn't invited me to her house, which got me away from all the drinking, I may never have left and then I would have been living in squats and on the streets, just like most of the people I was hanging out with. If I ever lived in New Orleans, I'd be dead within a few years, for sure.

New Orleans Merry-go-round

Lyrics:

I landed in New Orleans
First stop was India House
Next stop was Bourbon Street
From bar to bar I'd bounce

My home 'came Marie Laveau
The bar girls my new friends
They gave me an education
In music, voodoo, zen

I scared Lucy Lawless by wanting a straw
Without it princess I'd drop my beer on the floor
Lara and Candice provide me with free drinks
I made an impression there, that's what I think

I'm in New Orleans and I'm running wild
To say that I'm wasted is putting it mild
Keep this up, won't be long till I cark it
I love drinking that Southern Comfort

At night in Jackson Square
The psychics came out in force
The tarot told me my future
Of a beautiful woman, of course

I did meet such a lady
Willow was her name
She showed me around the city
The girl was clearly insane

And Willow wants sex in the house of God
Amen sister, if only we could
The fortune teller thinks that I'm Irish
Now when I see him I make my accent switch

I'm in New Orleans and I'm running wild
To say that I'm wasted is putting it mild
Keep this up, won't be long till I cark it
I love drinking that Southern Comfort

Will I ever get off this merry-go-round?
How will I escape this party town?
I'm gonna have to use a lifeline now
I wanna be running when I hit the ground

I'm in New Orleans and I'm running wild
To say that I'm wasted is putting it mild
Keep this up, won't be long till I cark it
I love drinking that Southern Comfort

But I met two friends in Rebecca and Jainie
And with their resources,
they were able to save me
I love the good times and perspective
they gave me
I jumped on a bus and I headed for DC

www.ingramcontent.com/pod-product-compliance
Lightning Source LLC
Chambersburg PA
CBHW070952080526
44587CB00015B/2280